Viola

T0080933

SIX VERY EASY PIECES

Op. 22

EDWARD ELGAR

BOSWORTH

Order No. BOE003913-01

SIX VERY EASY PIECES

Op. 22

EDWARD ELGAR

1.

Andante

2.

Allegretto

3.

Andante

4.

Andantino

5.

Allegretto
p
cresc.
f
dim.
p
4
cresc.
f dim.
p
4
cresc.
1
4
f
p dim.
2
4
f
p dim.

6.

Allegro
f
p
4
1
4
2
f
rit.
Fine

Cello

SIX VERY EASY PIECES

Op. 22

EDWARD ELGAR

BOSWORTH

Order No. BOE003913-02

SIX VERY EASY PIECES

Op. 22

EDWARD ELGAR

1.

Andante

2.

Allegretto

3.

Andante

4.

Andantino

5.

Allegretto

6.

Allegro